Stop Wishing, Start Doing.

Max Carey

ISBN: 9798367560251

DEDICATION

All progress takes place outside your comfort zone.

This book is dedicated to the action takers. .

CONTENTS

1 INTRODUCTION

Welcome to the world of fitness and working out! As a man, you have unique needs when it comes to working out and achieving your fitness goals. This book will provide you with comprehensive information on how to design workout plans that are tailored to your specific needs and goals and will provide a wide range of exercises and programs that you can use to reach your goals. With the right plan, you can make great strides in your health and fitness and look and feel your best.

This book is designed to provide a comprehensive overview of the basics of working out, as well as the different types of exercises and programs that are available for men. We'll start with a discussion of the basics of working out, including proper form and technique, safety considerations, and the benefits of working out. We'll also discuss the various types of training available, such as strength training, cardio, and cross-training. Finally, we'll discuss how to stay motivated and stick to your plans over the long term.

No matter what your fitness goals are, this book will provide you with the information and guidance you need to reach them.

We'll be discussing the importance of setting realistic goals. Knowing what you want to achieve and setting achievable goals is essential to staying motivated and achieving success. We'll discuss different types of goals and how to set them, as well as how to track your progress and adjust when necessary. We'll also discuss the importance of creating a healthy lifestyle, including good nutrition and rest.

Diving into the different types of exercises and programs available to men. We'll discuss the different types of strength training exercises, as well as cardio and cross-training. We'll discuss how to choose the right exercises for your specific goals, as well as how to create a workout plan that will help you reach those goals. We'll also discuss how to monitor your progress and adjust when necessary.

Finally, we'll discuss how to stay motivated and stick to your plan over the long term. We'll discuss how to stay focused, find ways to stay motivated, and how to stay on top of your plan even when faced with obstacles. We'll also talk about the importance of rest, recovery, and rest days. By the end of this book, you will have a comprehensive understanding of how to create and stick to a successful workout plan that is tailored to your individual needs and goals. With the right plan and the right attitude, you can make great strides in your health and fitness and look and feel your best.

2 BASICS OF WORKING OUT

This chapter will provide you with a comprehensive overview of the basics of working out. We'll discuss proper form and technique, safety considerations, and the benefits of working out. We'll also discuss the different types of training available, such as strength training, cardio, and cross-training.

Proper Form and Technique

Proper form and technique are essential when working out. Not only does proper form help you get the most out of your workouts, but it also helps to prevent injuries. When performing any exercise, make sure to keep your back straight, your head up, and your core engaged. Also, make sure to use a full range of motion for each exercise.

Having proper form and technique is key to any successful workout program. When you have proper form, you maximize the effectiveness of each exercise, allowing you to get the most out of your workout. Additionally, proper form and technique help reduce the risk of injury, as you're less likely to strain a muscle or pull a tendon with proper form. To ensure proper form and technique, make sure to keep your back straight, your head up and your core engaged when performing any exercise. Additionally, take the time to ensure that you are using a full range of motion for each exercise. Doing so will help you maximize the effectiveness of each exercise and reduce the risk of injury. As you get more familiar with the exercises you're performing, be sure to focus on proper form and technique to get the most out of your workouts.

Breathing Techniques

Breathing techniques are often overlooked when it comes to working out, yet they are an important factor when it comes to optimizing your performance. Proper breathing can help you get the most out of every workout and help you recover faster. Here are some tips to help you get the most out of your breathing while exercising. 1. Slow and Steady: Breathing slowly and steadily is key to getting the most out of your workout. When you're doing cardio, try to take a full breath in and out for every step or stroke. This will ensure that you're getting enough oxygen to your muscles without overdoing it. 2. Time It Right: Timing your breathing is also important. When lifting weights, it's best to exhale on the hardest part of the lift. This will give you more power and control so you can lift heavier weights. On the other hand, when doing cardio, try to inhale when your foot hits the ground and exhale when your foot leaves the ground. 3. Prioritize Your Core: Core breathing is essential for any type of exercise. When you're doing strength training, take a deep breath into your abdomen and hold it for a few seconds before exhaling. This will help you stabilize your core and improve your performance. 4. Visualize the Process: Visualizing the process of breathing can also be helpful. Try to imagine the air entering your lungs and being spread throughout your entire body. This will help you focus on the task at hand and ensure that you're breathing properly. 5. Breathe Through Your Nose: Finally, it's important to note that you should always breathe through your nose rather than your mouth. This will help you regulate the air flow and reduce any potential strain on your lungs. By following these tips, you should be able to get the most out of your breathing while working out. Remember, proper breathing can make a huge difference in your performance and recovery time, so make sure you're taking the time to focus on your breathing technique.

Safety Considerations

Safety should always be a priority when working out. Make sure to warm up and cool down properly before and after each workout, and always stretch to help prevent injuries. It's also important to listen to your body and take breaks when needed. Finally, make sure to use the proper form and technique when performing any exercise. Whether you're a novice or experienced exerciser, safety should always be a priority. From proper form and technique to warm-ups and cool-downs, there are a few safety considerations to keep in mind before and after your workouts.

Warm-Ups and Cool-Downs

One of the most important safety considerations when working out is to warm-up and cool-down properly. A dynamic warm-up, which includes activities such as jumping jacks, high-knees, and butt-kickers, helps to get your body ready for exercise by increasing the heart rate and raising the body temperature. After your workout, a cool-down helps to gradually slow your heart rate and reduce muscle soreness. Make sure to include stretching in both your warm-ups and cool-downs to help prevent injuries.

Listen to Your Body

It's important to recognize when your body needs a break. If you're feeling pain or your muscles are shaking, it's time to rest. It's also important to make sure you're getting enough rest in between workouts. Rest days are just as important as workout days and can help to reduce the risk of injury and burnout.

Benefits of Working Out

Working out provides a wide range of benefits, both physical and mental. Regular exercise can help to improve your strength, endurance, and cardiovascular health, as well as help to reduce stress and improve your overall mood. In addition, regular exercise can help to improve your sleep quality, as well as help to maintain a healthy weight.

Regular exercise provides a wide range of benefits, both physical and mental. From improved strength and endurance, to reduced stress and improved overall mood, here are some of the many benefits of working out.

Improved Strength and Endurance

Regular exercise can help to improve your strength and endurance. Strength training can help to build lean muscle mass and improve your overall strength, while aerobic exercise can help to improve your cardiovascular health and endurance.

Reduced Stress

Exercise can help to reduce stress levels by releasing endorphins, which are chemicals in the brain that act as natural painkillers and create feelings of euphoria. Exercise can also help to take your mind off your worries and provide a distraction from stressful situations.

Improved Mood

Regular exercise can help to improve your overall mood. Exercise helps to reduce stress, which can help to improve your mood. In addition, exercise can also help to increase your self-confidence and self-esteem.

Better Sleep Quality

Exercising regularly can help to improve your sleep quality. Exercise helps to tire out the body and make it easier to fall asleep. In addition, regular exercise can help to reduce stress, which can help to improve sleep quality.

Weight Maintenance

Exercise can help to maintain a healthy weight. Regular exercise helps to burn calories and keep your metabolism up, which can help with weight maintenance. In addition, exercise can help to improve your overall health, which can help to reduce the risk of obesity and other health-related issues.

Working out provides a wide range of benefits, both physical and mental. Regular exercise can help to improve your strength, endurance, and cardiovascular health, as well as help to reduce stress and improve your overall mood. In addition, regular exercise can help to improve your sleep quality, as well as help to maintain a healthy weight.

3 STRENGTH TRAINING FOR MEN

This chapter will provide you with an overview of strength training for men. We'll discuss different types of exercises, such as weightlifting and bodyweight exercises, as well as the benefits of strength training. We'll also discuss different types of programs and how to design a program that is tailored to your individual needs and goals.

Types of Exercises

Strength training exercises can be divided into two categories: weightlifting and bodyweight exercises. Weightlifting exercises involve the use of barbells, dumbbells, and other weight training equipment. Bodyweight exercises involve using your own bodyweight as resistance, such as push-ups and pull-ups.

Weightlifting Exercises

Weightlifting exercises are a great way to build strength and muscle size. Barbell exercises, such as squats and deadlifts, are some of the most effective exercises for increasing strength. Dumbbell exercises, such as bicep curls and triceps extensions, are also effective for building strength. Other weight training equipment, such as kettlebells, medicine balls, and cable machines, can also be used to build strength.

Bodyweight Exercises

Bodyweight exercises are a great way to build strength and muscle without the need for any additional equipment. Push-ups, pull-ups, and bodyweight squats are some of the most effective bodyweight exercises for building strength. Other bodyweight exercises, such as planks, burpees, and mountain climbers, can also be used to build strength and muscle. Both weightlifting and bodyweight exercises can be effective for building strength and muscle. The type of exercise you choose should depend on your goals and personal preferences. If you're looking to build strength and muscle size, then weightlifting exercises are a great choice. If you're looking for a more convenient way to build strength and muscle, then bodyweight exercises are a great choice.

Weightlifting exercises are great for building strength and muscle size. For example, the squat is one of the most effective exercises for building lower body strength and size. Other weightlifting exercises, such as bench press, deadlifts, and overhead press, are also great for building overall strength and muscle size. Weightlifting exercises can also be used to target specific muscle groups, such as biceps and triceps. Bodyweight exercises are great for building strength and muscle without the need for any additional equipment. Push-ups, pull-ups, and bodyweight squats are some of the most effective bodyweight exercises for building strength.

Other bodyweight exercises, such as planks, burpees, and mountain climbers, can also be used to build strength and muscle. Bodyweight exercises are also convenient and can be done anywhere, anytime, making them a great choice for those who travel frequently. Overall, both weightlifting and bodyweight exercises can be effective for building strength and muscle. The type of exercise you choose should depend on your goals and personal preferences. If you're looking for a convenient way to build strength and muscle, then bodyweight exercises are a great choice. If you're looking to build strength and muscle size, then weightlifting exercises are a great choice.

Types of Programs

There are a variety of different types of strength training programs available. These include full-body programs, split programs, and periodization programs. A full-body program involves working all major muscle groups in each workout, while a split program involves focusing on different muscle groups in different workouts. Periodization programs involve varying the type and intensity of exercises over time. There are several different types of workouts splits you can use. The most popular splits include the full body split, upper/lower split, push/pull split, and body part split. The full body split consists of exercises for all muscle groups in one workout. This is a great choice for people who don't have a lot of time or who are just starting out. The upper/lower split divides your workouts into upper body and lower body exercises. This allows you to target specific muscle groups with more intensity.

A push pull legs split is a type of weight training split where the exercises are divided into three distinct groups – push, pull, and legs. The push exercises are those that work the muscles involved in pushing motions, such as chest, shoulders, and triceps. The pull exercises are those that work the muscles involved in pulling motions, such as back and biceps. Finally, the leg exercises are those that work the muscles in the legs, such as the quadriceps, hamstrings, and glutes. Each muscle group is worked with a separate workout. For example, a typical push workout might include exercises such as bench press, shoulder press, and triceps extensions. A typical pull workout might include exercises such as lat pulldowns, rows, and bicep curls. A typical leg workout might include exercises such as squats, lunges, and calf raises. The main advantage of a push pull legs split is that it allows for more frequent training of each muscle group. This is because each muscle group is trained on its own day, allowing for more rest and recovery in between workouts. Additionally, this type of split allows for more focus on each muscle group and more variety in exercises.

Overall, the push pull legs split is a great way to maximize muscle growth and strength gains. It is especially useful for those who are short on time and can't devote multiple days to weight training. Which split you choose will depend on your goals, experience level, and schedule. If you want to build muscle, the body part split may be a good option. If you're looking for more of a general fitness routine, the full body split may work best. No matter which split you choose, it's important to ensure that you're getting enough rest and recovery between workouts. This will help you avoid injury and maximize your results. Splitting up your workouts can be a great way to get the most out of your training. Try different splits to find what works best for you.

Designing Programs

When designing a program, it's important to consider your individual needs and goals. Start by determining how much time you have available to commit to your workouts, as well as the type of equipment that you have access to. Once you have this information, you can choose exercises and create a program that is tailored to your individual needs and goals.

4 CARDIO WORKOUTS FOR MEN

This chapter will provide you with an overview of cardio workouts for men. We'll discuss different types of cardio exercises, as well as the benefits of cardio workouts. We'll also discuss different types of programs and how to design a program that is tailored to your individual needs and goals.

Types of Exercises

Cardio exercises can be divided into two categories: aerobic exercises and anaerobic exercises. Aerobic exercises involve sustained, low-intensity activities that increase your heart rate, such as jogging, biking, and swimming. Anaerobic exercises involve short bursts of intense activity, such as sprinting and interval training.

Aerobic Exercises

Aerobic exercises are any type of exercise that increases your heart rate and breathing for an extended period. Examples of aerobic exercises include jogging, biking, swimming, and walking. These activities help improve your cardiovascular health by strengthening your heart and lungs. Additionally, aerobic exercises can help you burn fat, as your body needs to use more energy to sustain the activity for an extended period.

Anaerobic Exercises

Anaerobic exercises are any type of exercises that involve short bursts of intense activity, such as sprinting, jumping, or weightlifting. These activities require your body to use energy without the presence of oxygen, meaning that they are more intense than aerobic exercises. While they may not be as effective at burning fat, they can help you build muscle and improve your strength.

Benefits of Cardio

Cardio workouts provide many benefits to your cardiovascular health. Regular aerobic exercise helps to improve your heart health, as well as strengthen your heart muscles. This helps to reduce your risk of heart disease and stroke. In addition, it can help to lower your blood pressure and cholesterol levels, as well as reduce the risk of developing type 2 diabetes.

Cardio workouts also help to burn fat, which can help you to reach your weight loss goals. Regular aerobic exercise can help to increase your metabolism, which can help to boost your calorie burn throughout the day. This can help to reduce your overall body fat percentage and help you to look and feel your best.

Cardio workouts can help to improve your endurance and stamina, which can help to improve your performance in physical activities. Regular aerobic exercise can help to increase your oxygen capacity, which can help you to last longer during physical activities. This can also help to reduce your risk of injury.

Cardio workouts can also help to reduce stress and improve your overall mood. Exercise can help to reduce levels of stress hormones in the body, and can help to reduce feelings of anxiety and depression. Regular aerobic exercise can also help to release endorphins, which are the hormones that are responsible for making you feel good.

Overall, cardio workouts can provide a wide range of health benefits. Regular aerobic exercise can help to improve your cardiovascular health, as well as help to burn fat and increase your metabolism. In addition, cardio workouts can help to improve your endurance and stamina, and can help to reduce stress and improve your overall mood.

3.3 Types of Programs There are a variety of different types of cardio programs available. These include interval training, circuit training, and steady-state cardio. Interval training involves alternating between periods of high-intensity exercise and periods of rest. Circuit training involves performing a series of exercises with little to no rest in between. Steady-state cardio involves performing a continuous exercise at a moderate intensity for an extended period.

Interval Training

Interval training is one of the most popular types of cardio programs. This involves alternating between periods of high-intensity exercise and periods of rest. During the high-intensity periods, you should work hard enough that it is difficult to keep up the intensity for more than a few minutes. During the rest period, you should slow down or stop exercising completely. Interval training is great for improving fitness and burning more calories in a short amount of time.

Circuit Training

Circuit training is a type of training where you perform a series of exercises with little to no rest in between. For example, you might perform 10 minutes of burpees followed by 10 minutes of mountain climbers and then 10 minutes of jumping jacks. This type of training allows you to work multiple muscle groups at once and can be done in a shorter amount of time than traditional cardio.

Steady-State Cardio

Steady-state cardio involves performing a continuous exercise at a moderate intensity for an extended period. Examples of steady-state cardio include walking, jogging, cycling, and swimming. This type of cardio is great for burning calories and improving overall fitness. It is also a great way to increase your aerobic capacity. No matter what type of cardio program you choose, it is important to remember to listen to your body and make sure you are not overdoing it. In addition, make sure to eat a healthy diet and get enough rest to maximize your results.

Designing Programs

When designing a program, it's important to consider your individual needs and goals. Start by determining how much time you have available to commit to your workouts, as well as the type and intensity of exercises that you are comfortable with. Once you have this information, you can choose exercises and create a program that is tailored to your individual needs and goals.

5 CROSS TRAINING FOR MEN

Cross-training for men has become an increasingly popular way to stay in shape, build muscle, and increase overall health. Cross-training is a form of exercise that combines different types of activity, such as running, swimming, and weight training, to improve physical fitness and overall health. This type of exercise is beneficial for men of all ages, as it can help them become stronger, improve coordination, and balance, and reduce stress.

One of the main benefits of cross-training for men is its ability to improve strength and muscle tone. By engaging in a variety of activities, men can target different muscle groups and improve their overall strength. Cross-training can also help men build muscle faster than traditional weight training alone. This is because different activities recruit different muscle fibers, allowing for greater overall muscle development.

In addition to improved strength, cross-training can also help men improve coordination and balance. By engaging in different activities, men can gain a better understanding of their body and how it moves. This can help them better handle activities like sports, hiking, and various other activities that require balance and coordination.

Cross-training can also help men reduce stress. By engaging in different activities, men can break away from their daily routine and focus on something that is enjoyable. This change of pace can help men relax and clear their minds, allowing them to approach life with a fresh perspective.

Finally, cross-training is beneficial for men because it can help them prevent injuries. By participating in different activities, men can help reduce the risk of overuse injuries, which are caused by repeating the same activity repeatedly. This can help men stay healthy and active, which is important for their overall health and well-being.

Types of Exercises Cross

The four main types of cross training are aerobic, anaerobic, resistance, and balance. Each type of cross training provides unique benefits and can be used to customize a fitness program to fit individual goals.

Aerobic activities involve activities that increase the heart rate and breathing rate for a sustained period. Examples of aerobic activities include running, cycling, swimming, and rowing. Aerobic activities are great for developing cardiovascular endurance and improving overall fitness.

Anaerobic activities involve activities that require

quick bursts of energy. Examples of anaerobic activities include sprinting, weightlifting, and jumping. Anaerobic activities are great for developing strength and power.

Resistance training involves activities that use resistance to challenge muscles and improve strength. Examples of resistance activities include weightlifting, Pilates, and yoga. Resistance training is great for improving strength and muscle tone.

Balance exercises involve activities that challenge balance and coordination. Examples of balance exercises include Pilates, yoga, and tai chi. Balance exercises are great for improving stability and balance.

Designing a Cross Training program

When designing a program, it's important to consider your individual needs and goals. Start by determining how much time you have available to commit to your workouts, as well as the type and intensity of exercises that you are comfortable with. Once you have this information, you can choose exercises and create a program that is tailored to your individual needs and goals.

1. Start slow: Before beginning any new exercise program, it's important to ease into it. Start with simple exercises and movements that are familiar to you.
2. Have a plan: It's important to have an idea of what exercises you are going to do and how often. A good plan will include a variety of activities that focus on different muscle groups and intensity levels.

3. Monitor your progress: Keep track of your progress, such as how many reps you can do or how far you run. This will help you measure your progress and hold yourself accountable.
4. Change it up: Make sure to mix up your routine every few weeks to avoid boredom and overuse injuries.
5. Listen to your body: Don't push yourself too hard. Pay attention to warning signs from your body, such as pain or fatigue, and adjust your workouts accordingly.
6. Seek professional help: If you're unsure of how to properly execute exercises or create a plan, consider hiring a personal trainer or joining a class.

6 TIPS FOR STAYING MOTIVATED

This chapter will provide you with tips for staying motivated when working out. We'll discuss how to set realistic goals, how to track your progress, and how to stay motivated over the long term.

Staying motivated in the gym can be a challenge for many people. With the constant temptation to skip your workout and the difficulty of seeing results, it can be hard to stay motivated and keep going. However, there are some simple tips that can help you stay motivated and make the most of your gym time.

Start by making small changes to your routine. Try changing the order of your exercises or adding a new exercise to your routine. This will give you something new to focus on and help keep you motivated.

Set realistic goals for yourself and make sure to

reward yourself when you achieve them. This will give you something to strive for and help keep you motivated.

Find a workout buddy who can help keep you accountable. Working out with a friend can make it more fun and keep you motivated.

Listen to music while you work out. Music has been proven to improve performance and can help keep you motivated.

Finally, take some time to reflect on your progress. Seeing the progress, you've made can be a great motivator and give you the confidence to keep going.

Staying motivated in the gym can be a challenge, but it is possible. By making small changes to your routine, setting realistic goals, finding a workout buddy, listening to music, and reflecting on your progress, you can stay motivated and make the most of your time in the gym. On yourself if you miss a workout.

7 CONCLUSION

Working out is an important part of staying healthy and looking and feeling your best. With the right plan, you can make great strides in your health and fitness and reach your goals. This book has provided you with a comprehensive overview of the basics of working out, as well as different types of exercises and programs that are available for men. Now that you have this information, you are ready to start designing and following workout plans that are tailored to your individual needs and goals.

In addition to the information provided in this book, there are many other helpful resources available to help you on your path to a healthier lifestyle. Working out with a partner or group of friends can be an effective way to stay motivated, and there are a variety of online communities and support systems that can help you stay on track. You can also consult with a personal trainer or nutritionist to help create a plan that works best for you. With dedication and perseverance, you can achieve your fitness goals and live a healthier life.

YouTube is another great resource for men looking to get fit. There are a variety of channels dedicated to men's fitness, offering advice on everything from proper form to nutrition and supplementation. These channels offer instructional videos, workout plans, and even live streams of workouts. Many of these channels are run by fitness professionals, so you can be sure you're getting reliable information. YouTube also provides a supportive community, with comments and discussions that can help keep you motivated and accountable. With the right combination of guidance and dedication, YouTube can be an invaluable tool to help you reach your fitness goals.

In conclusion, fitness for men is a journey that can be both rewarding and challenging. Men of all ages and backgrounds can achieve their fitness goals with hard work and dedication. The benefits of regular exercise, a balanced diet, and a healthy lifestyle are numerous and include improved emotional and physical health, increased energy, and a better sense of self-worth. Men should remember to set realistic goals and stick to a consistent routine to ensure the best results. With the right attitude and approach, any man can reach his fitness goals and be proud of his accomplishments.

NOTES

Stop wishing, Start Doing.

Stop wishing, Start Doing.

Stop wishing, Start Doing.

Stop wishing, Start Doing.

Stop wishing, Start Doing.

www.ingramcontent.com/pod-product-compliance
Lightning Source LLC
LaVergne TN
LVHW020529160826
845677LV00015B/3977